Also by David DeFord

Make Your Life a Masterpiece

1000 Brilliant Leadership Quotes

I Wish to Be Useful

Ordinary People Can Achieve Their Lofty Goals

Ordinary People Can Self-Publish Big Sellers

Ordinary People Can Earn Huge Web Profits

Where Seldom Is Heard a Discouraging Word

1000 Brilliant Achievement Quotes

Ordinary People Can Achieve the Extraordinary

Hippie Serendipity: A Story of Peace, Love, and Freedom

Good News about Business Networking

David DeFord

Ordinary People Can Win! Omaha, Nebraska

10 9 8 7 6 5 4 3 2
David DeFord Creative Consulting
13964 Margo Street
Omaha, NE 68138
david@daviddeford.com

David DeFord is dedicated to helping small business people with big dreams and tiny budgets attract more clients.

He teaches his clients and audiences low cost, high producing marketing methods. His *Almost Free Marketing* presentations simplify the maze of marketing, networking, and social media.

David's blog, DavidDeFord.com, provides excellent information on the latest low cost marketing opportunities.

To book David for your convention or annual meeting, e-mail him at david@daviddeford.com.
You can find the author on the following social media:
LinkedIn: LinkedIn.com/in/daviddeford
Twitter: @DavidDeFord

About the Author

David helps entrepreneurs, independent professionals, and sales executives who have big dreams and tiny budgets.

His clients enjoy tremendous business growth as they learn to focus on first things first. He helps them achieve their long-held goals.

His audiences and clients come away from his presentations with useful tips and strategies to help them attract more referrals and sales. They learn how to make their entire networking experience delightful for themselves and for their contacts.

He does this through entertaining training classes for organizations, public workshops, and speeches. He promises fresh information presented in an entertaining style.

David is an award-winning speaker with thousands of speeches under his belt. He received the highest communicator award from Toastmasters International and is a member of the National Speakers Association.

He has fourteen published books on personal development themes.

Acknowledgments

I thank my Friday morning networking group:
Gerry Phelan, Dan Weber, Bid Taylor, Chuck King ,
Terri Smejia, and Nancy Kirk.

Thank you for teaching me about joining friendship
and business.

Table of Contents

Chapter One

Good News about Business Networking

Business networking can be your most fruitful and enjoyable activity for attracting new business. It can also be an uncomfortable, terrifying, and useless waste of time. Which is it for you?

If you attend several networking events a month and never seem to attract any clients with your efforts, you need the information in *Good News about Business Networking*. This book will also help you if you are one of the many people who sit in your car working up your courage to go inside to the event.

You may feel disappointed at your poor results. You may feel shy about talking about yourself or your product to strangers. You may wish you knew what to say or how to turn these conversations into business growth.

I have good news. You can turn your discomfort into pleasure. You can begin to attract scores of new referrals and clients from the people you meet at networking events.

Business networking success is not complicated. It's simple and it's enjoyable.

In this guide you will learn that selling at networking events never works. You will read how providing value to another person BEFORE you ask for their help will produce more referrals. You will learn how concentrating on *giving* rather than *getting* works. You will also learn that how you follow up with your contacts makes all the difference.

So chill out. Take a few deep, cleansing breaths, and learn the *Good News about Business Networking*.

Good News Summary

1. Shyness and fear need not slow down your networking efforts.

2. You can enjoy the process.

3. It's not complicated nor costly to attract referrals.

Chapter Two

Networking Is Not Selling

Novice networkers get confused. They enter a room filled with business people of all stripes. They see men dressed in black business suits or women in red skirts and jackets. Others wear polo shirts and khakis. I've even seen attendees in pajamas and night hats. Attendees serve in different industries: bankers, financial planners, insurance agents, realtors, carpet cleaners, business coaches, consultants, and every other industry.

When the novice networker enters the event she sees a room filled with sales prospects. **That idea-selling at networking events--is the cardinal sin of business networking.** Word that you're selling spreads fast around the hall.

At one event a friend alerted me, "See the guy in the blue shirt? He's hard-selling." A few minutes later, someone else gave me the same warning. When I sat down to eat some finger food, our aggressive salesman sat next to me. He proceeded to ask personal questions about my identification protection. He pushed and prodded with as little finesse as a prizefighter.

When experienced networkers enter a room filled with other businesspeople, they see the hall filled with potential *referral sources,* not potential sales prospects. If 100 people attend and event, and those 100 know 250 each. You are staring at 25,000 potential referrals.

The advanced networker knows this important fact:

Networking is all about building and nurturing new business relationships that will result in lasting friendships and scores of referrals.

It's all about building goodwill. You want people to think of you first when they know someone who needs your product or service. When they see that you are phoning them or that they have an e-mail from you, you want them to smile inside and welcome the contact. When they see you at networking events, you want them to eagerly introduce you to their other friends. Once you have a few dozen friends who feel this way toward you, the referrals will flow.

Building these relationships and feelings of goodwill will happen in several stages:

- At networking events

- In your *immediate* follow up after the event

- As you touch base with them periodically

- And as you interact with them online

Once you've learned this important fact about building goodwill versus selling, you will attract tremendous numbers of referrals. Plus, after a little practice, you will lose all of your fear and begin to enjoy your networking experiences.

Good News Summary

1. Sales skills aren't needed for effective networking.

2. Each person you meet represents about 250 potential referrals.

3. Building goodwill is the key and isn't difficult.

Chapter Three

At the Event

So here you are at a chamber of commerce networking event. As you walk in you see about 150 people dressed in assorted levels of business attire milling around. They seem to be clustered in groups of two, three, or even six people. They all seem so at ease. They even seem to be enjoying themselves. Are they faking? Do they belong to some brainwashed cult? Have they done this for years and grown accustomed to the unpleasant task of networking?

Good news: They aren't part of a cult but they do know some secrets you probably don't.Here are a few of those secrets:

- They aren't there to make sales, their goal is to make acquaintances

- They don't push their contacts IN ANY WAY

- They do everything they can to make the people with whom they talk enjoy the conversation by getting them to speak about themselves

- They avoid negative topics like: war, disasters, and the latest political idiocy (it's tough I know)

- Rather, they get their contacts to talk about their businesses, their families, and their passions

- They care more about RECEIVING business cards than they do about GIVING them out

- In reverse, they focus on GIVING value to their contacts rather than on RECEIVING from them

People love to talk about themselves, especially if you lead and encourage them. Asking a few good questions will leave them feeling you are the greatest conversationalist ever.

If you have focused your discussion on their businesses, their challenges, and their passions, they will welcome your follow up phone calls and e-mails.

They will gladly introduce their friends to you because they know you will treat their buddies with the same respect that you treated them. Those introductions bring the gold.

What questions can you ask to help start a good business relationship? Here are a few suggestions that will give you the idea:

- What do you do?

- How did you get started in your business?

- What do you enjoy most about your profession?

- What separates you and your company from your competitors?

- What advice would you give someone just starting in your industry?

- What significant changes have you seen take place in your profession through the years? (Especially effective if the contact has graying temples)

- What do you see as coming trends in your industry?

- What ways have you found to be the most effective for promoting your business?

- How can I know if someone I'm talking to is a good prospect for you?

Be careful to exclude these barriers to bonding: jargon, pressure, and too much focus on you.

Looking a person in the eye shows that you're focused solely on them. It shows respect and interest. Avoid looking over their shoulder searching for better people to approach. Stay in the moment with your new contact.

Good News Summary

1. You can be one of those cool and confident networkers.

2. No pushing is necessary.

3. You don't have to talk about yourself.

4. Contacts who enjoy talking with you gladly accept follow up invitations.

Chapter Four

Find Common Ground

Strong connections are made when two parties find that they have important things in common. Search for the common ground.

My friend Rick and I met at a networking event and found that we both loved the Boston Red Sox. That common interest has deepened our friendship and given us some good opening conversation each time we see other. We always light up when we meet.

Ask about your contacts' passions and pastimes. Did your former careers cross paths? Do they know some of the same people as you? Did they once live near your hometown or in a city where you once resided?

Later we'll discuss other ways to find common ground using *LinkedIn*.

Good News Summary

1. Finding common ground is simple and quick.

Chapter Five

Be the Host

If the person you meet at a networking event hasn't attended many functions, become their host. Take them around the room and introduce them to some of your other friends. Where possible, help them meet potential prospects or people who offer resources that may solve your new friend's current challenge.

Once you've introduced them to a few of your friends, shake their hand and leave them with a trusted colleague. You need not spend your entire time hosting new acquaintances. They will be grateful for the help you've offered them. Plan to send a follow up later the same day. We'll discuss follow up methods later.

Find the Right People
I look for two types of people to meet at networking events--centers of influence and those who look really afraid.

Centers of influence are those who know many of the people in the room. They usually have a small crowd around them because others know the value of their influence.

These connected people pass referrals liberally. They know how to match people.

Scared people feel so grateful when you relieve them of the responsibility of finding people with whom to speak.

Learn about their businesses and generate goodwill with them. Be their host. Help them make connections. Good will come of it.

Good Places to Stand

I've found that three places serve as the best positions for meeting new people: the entrance, near the food, and near the trash receptacle.

Standing in these posts you can greet nearly every attendee.

How to Penetrate a Group

I prefer networking events where I can sit at a table with several other attendees. I look for a table where I know fewer people. But many functions are "stand up" events where you must roam around looking for someone to meet. This can make even a veteran networker squirm.

With whom should I talk? How do I join an existing cluster of networkers comfortably?

Here's my approach. I walk up to the circle and stand just behind and between two participants. I wait a few seconds. Usually, the two will notice me and move aside so I can join them. If not, I put my hand on one's shoulder and introduce myself. I've never had a bad experience or rude reaction. They are there to make friends and build goodwill also.

Set "Five and Five" Goals
I always have two goals to achieve when I attend a function. I never let myself leave an event until I've reached them. They're not difficult, and usually only take an hour or so to achieve.

I have pleasant conversations with five new people and I collect all five of their business cards.

This works. It works very well. **IF** you follow up effectively. I'll discuss later some options for follow up, but I want to stress here that you will rarely make meaningful and fruitful business relationships if you rely solely on your work at networking events.

Follow up is key.
Setting "Five and Five" goals will relieve you of the pressure to come away from the functions with several people pre-sold on your products. You go in, get your five and five, and you leave.

How to Shake a Leech
I'm often asked how I extract myself from someone who wants to dominate my time. It's not too tough.

Spending ten minutes with a person at an event is enough. After that you're losing precious time and achieving no additional benefits for you or for your contact.

I always remind myself that I have my goals for the event. I want to have five pleasant conversations with new contacts and I collect their business cards. If I'm stuck with one person who may or may not be a potential networking friend, I'll lose the opportunity to reach my two goals. So I've developed a few methods for extracting myself from a clinger.

The Hand-off
As I find myself stuck in a conversation that isn't going anywhere, I sometimes grab someone I know who is walking by and introduce the leech to them. After a few seconds of conversation I leave the two alone so they can get better acquainted. Does that create bad will? I don't think so. Those two may really hit it off. I never use this approach in trying to pry away an aggressive seller. Those I confront and try to re-educate.

The Bladder Strategy
Another way to shake a leech is to let them know you need to hit the restroom now or you may leave a puddle on the nice carpet. Not a bad strategy, but occasionally the person follows me into the bathroom.

Make sure you do have to relieve yourself if you try this approach. Drink lots of water.

The Fake Phone Call
If you don't mind being untruthful you could say your phone is buzzing and you need to get it. The rooms

are so loud with busy networkers that the leech would never hear it anyway. If you have an iPhone you have it made, "There's an app for that." The apps initiate phone calls when you need to leave a long meeting or extract a leech.

If I met you at a networking event and handed you off, left to go to the restroom, or answered a buzzing mobile phone--I'm really sorry.

Remember, the "Five and Five" strategy at networking events: have five pleasant conversations with new contacts and get all five of their business cards.

Create Goodwill

Always remember that your job at networking events is to establish goodwill. You attend these functions so you can help at least five people feel good about their visit with you. This puts you in a position to receive more welcome receptions when you follow up.

Unfortunately, many networkers destroy that goodwill by refusing to follow the rules of the event. If you are are a speaker and are asked to speak for three minutes but continue your talk for five, you've damage your goodwill.

The most common rule violated is when everyone is given the opportunity to introduce himself. If you're asked to only state your name and company name because of the large number of attendees, stick to the rules. You may feel tempted to include your clever byline or some other witty comment. Don't! Everyone else abides by the rule. If they do and you don't, you're seen as a cheater and will lose the goodwill you've worked hard to obtain.

There are much better ways to stand out.

I urge you to do everything in your power to create a positive brand by learning the protocol of each event and follow it carefully.

Good News Summary

1. Introduce your new friends to your older ones.

2. Centers of influence can match you with excellent prospects.

3. Scared people show their gratitude.

4. Simply have pleasant conversations with five new people and collect all five of their business cards.

5. Leeches are easily shaken.

6. You can create goodwill simply.

Chapter Six

What Networking Venues Should You Attend?

Where do frugal networkers go to find referral sources? Which venues provide the best fit for our needs? Here are some simple suggestions to help you find the most appropriate networking venues for you.

Chambers of Commerce

Most local chambers provide a variety of networking events designed to promote business exchange between its members. They offer:

- Early morning gatherings you can attend on the way to work,

- Late afternoon events for the trip home,

- Lunch and learn sessions,

- Business classes where participants can mingle before and after the session and during breaks,

- Ribbon cuttings for new businesses or locations,

- Golf outings, and

- Referral groups.

Chamber of Commerce events make great networking opportunities because everyone there intends to network for business purposes--that's why they came.

You can feel confident and even bold at these gatherings. That said--don't sell at the event. Use the principles taught earlier. Meet some new people, have pleasant conversations with them, and get their business cards.

Large metropolitan chambers help you connect with a wide array of contacts. I belong to the large chamber in my town and benefit from my involvement.

Smaller chambers, like the ones specific to a small section of town or a unique demographic (like ethnicity) are even better for these reasons:

- The dues are less than a third of those of the larger chambers

- You have instant common ground

- You'll enjoy a small town type of friendliness

- The bureaucracy is much less of a barrier

- You are more likely to be able to volunteer, make presentations, or find other ways to enhance your visibility

- Networking is one-on-one anyway, so smaller events are better for making strong connections

Before you join a chamber, I suggest you attend some of their events to get the feel for the organization.

Service Clubs
Most service clubs were originally formed to promote business exchange and to serve their communities. Some restrict membership to one member per position type. They only want one insurance agent, one financial planner, etc. Belonging to a service club provides a wonderful way for you to do good works while you serve side-by-side with potential referral sources.

Be aware, though, that many service clubs discourage open solicitation. If you follow the principles we discuss in this book, you'll be in line with their guidelines.

The pros of networking at service clubs include:

• Instant common ground

• Relationships deepen when you work side-by-side with others for a good cause

• When you volunteer for committees and leadership positions you increase your visibility and develop stronger relationships with your colleagues.

• You serve great causes while you network

• Since most clubs meet weekly, you get to know the other members closely

The cons:

- The membership dues can be astronomical

- Younger people haven't caught the vision of service clubs so a large number of members are retired

- Some clubs have minimum attendance requirements of 50% to 80%

Like with the chambers of commerce, I urge you to attend a few times before you lay out the cash for the dues. You want to make sure you meet your needs and goals BEFORE you toss away your money.

Referral and Tips Groups One popular method for gaining referrals is through close-knit groups designed for such exchange. Those involved meet each week, introduce themselves with short "commercials" and trade referrals furiously.

Many of my friends LOVE these groups. The entire focus is on passing and receiving referrals or tips. It's an effective means for attracting referrals. Many of these groups ask their members to carry their colleagues' business cards with them in case they find a decent referral in their daily course of business.

I encourage you to check out one of these groups. I must pass along one caution, however. My philosophy on giving referrals doesn't fit the referral group model. I give several referrals each week. I do it because it makes me happy--like giving unexpected gifts. I do it out of a sense of caring and loyalty, not out of duty or obligation. I also believe in most of the principles of the *Law of Attraction*--when I give out *good* without expectation, the universe returns *good* to me.

Giving referrals so that I can meet my obligations to a referral group ruins it for me. When I give referrals to satisfy a requirement, the focus is on my needs rather than on the needs of others. But that's just me.

Pros of referral groups:

- Deep relationships form as you serve each other

- The frequency of contact makes closer connections

- The quantity of referrals is great

Cons:

- Dues can be very stiff

- Some groups have minimum attendance requirements

- The quality of referrals is sometimes weak since members often try to think up referrals while they drive to the meeting

Classes, Conventions and Seminars
Attending seminars, conventions, and classes can result in very good networking opportunities. As you share the experiences of learning together, you tend to

develop relationships with other attendees. This is especially true when you take extended courses that meet in multiple sessions. Before and after the class and during breaks are excellent times to ask questions and get to know the other students.

Volunteering and Church Involvement
Working together on a good cause creates closeness. Since most of these experiences generate wonderful and deep feelings of joy, those with whom you labor become associated with those feelings.

The possibilities are endless, and include:

• Parent-Teacher organizations

• School committees

• Churches

• Youth athletics

• Health and wellness organizations, like the American Lung Association

• Special Olympics

• Environmental concerns

• Scouting

• Global relief, like Red Cross

• Big Brothers and Big Sisters

- Organizations serving the aged

- Humane society

- Groups serving veterans

Don't just attend meetings, roll up your sleeves and get involved. You need to watch less television anyway. Do some good and grow your business at the same time.

Host Your Own Networking Group
One last venue for quality networking is one you host yourself. Start small and let it grow naturally. You can promote it as you network at other venues; you can send paper or e-mail invitations; you can ask your connections to bring guests.

What's in it for you?

- You get to showcase your business

- You attract people to your facility (if you host it there)

- You control the agenda

- You enhance your connections' memories of you

My friend Hethe Berg and I hosted a biweekly SendOutCards Networking Lunch. In ninety minutes we eat lunch and enjoy a stress-free, no-pressure agenda.

Here's what we did:

- Everyone introduced themselves, told a little about their business and their ideal prospects

- If they used SendOutCards, they would tell how they used the cards to grow their businesses or they told a SendOutCards success story

- Hethe and I showed them how sending a card is as simple as sending an e-mail

- We explained how to get started.

In all, we spent only twenty minutes on SendOutCards to insure that the visitors enjoy a powerful venue for networking so they'll want to return.

You can do something similar. Be creative. Enjoy the role of a gracious host. People will remember you fondly.

Good News Summary

1. Smaller, regional chambers of commerce offer low cost alternatives to larger chambers.

2. Service clubs and volunteer opportunities help you attract referrals while you serve wonderful causes.

3. Mix learning and networking at seminars and classes.

4. Host your own networking group and get slightly famous.

Chapter Seven

Follow Up Effectively and Harvest Bountiful Referrals

Immediate and creative follow up will enhance the goodwill and friendly feelings you've engendered at networking events. When you follow up effectively you stand above the others. Most networkers rely on their savvy at networking events to create the desired effect. They feel that seeing people repeatedly at these functions generates enough goodwill. Not so.

The frequency of such contact does help. But when you follow up you stand well above the others. You show professionalism, discipline, and thoughtfulness.

Want to destroy goodwill in your follow up? Call them up and start selling to them or send them a form letter.

Rather, you want to enhance the goodwill they felt when they met you.

Want to underwhelm your contact? Send them a generic e-mail.

Wise networkers find more personal ways to strengthen their business relationships.

Schedule Time Immediately Following the Event
Rather than blocking out only the meeting time on your calendar, add another half hour so that you can immediately follow up. If you wait too long you won't remember anything from your conversation.

Also, you really stand out if you mail something out to them *that day*!

I always block out time following a networking event. It's a habit and a discipline. You're going to take the time anyway. You might as well do it early as opposed to late. You'll be more likely to get it done if you do it earlier and you'll strengthen the impact.

Phone Calls
I'll admit I have a personal bias against receiving phone follow up. Phone calls are intrusive. They hurt productivity. If I don't stop my project to answer the phone, I'm wondering who called and what opportunity awaits.

But putting my own prejudice aside, many other people feel less than receptive to phone calls. They dislike the interruption and they feel apprehensive about being put on the spot from an aggressive seller.

Such calls rarely nurture goodwill.

Voice mails regarding networking follow up rarely get returned.

E-mails

Sending an e-mail is free and very simple. It's quick. You can copy and paste the same message to everyone. Or you can blind copy everyone you met at the event. It's so easy that most people who follow up prefer this method.

Your contacts know that. They know that you put very little thought, no expense, and only seconds into your communication. You've underwhelmed them.

Such e-mails rarely get saved. They're briefly scanned and deleted immediately. At best, they'll send you a quick reply thanking you for the e-mail. If you write more than fifty words in your e-mail very few of your contacts will even read it.

E-mail follow up barely registers in the contacts' minds.

Voice mails rarely get returned and e-mails usually get deleted.

Personal Notes and Cards

If you want to greatly enhance the goodwill you've generated on meeting someone, follow up with a personal note or card.

You may sort your mail prior to opening it like I do. First, I open anything that looks like it may contain a check I've been expecting. Second, I open greeting cards. I know that anything in a card-sized envelope will never contain bad news. After that, the fun's over.

Next I open #10 business envelopes. I know that they usually contain sales letters, credit card offers (yes, I still get them), and other uninteresting stuff. Lastly, I look at postcards and other printed sales materials.

Checks and greeting cards are welcome one hundred percent of the time. In fact, you can send me either anytime you wish. My office address is: 13964 Margo Street, Omaha, NE 68138. My birthday is November 23rd. Send me a birthday card. I love receiving them. Don't you?

Greeting cards punch a more powerful blow when they're not expected and when there's no obligation attached. I'm pleased to get a birthday card from my mother. But she has to send me one. When people I meet through networking send me a card, I'm impressed.

Sending greeting cards to networking contacts has netted me more new consulting clients than radio advertising, phone calling, and public speaking combined. It works.

That said, I have some guidelines for you to make your card sending more powerful.

1. Don't send pre-printed, plainlooking Thank You cards. Boorriinngg!

2. Use language that is focused on your contact, not on yourself.

3. Do not ask for anything nor add any wording that implies that you're selling.

4. Use your own handwriting or use a system that prints in your own handwriting font.

5. Use blue ink rather than black. It looks less "photocopy-like."

6. Before sending the card, think, "If I were to receive this card, how long would I keep it?' Shoot for cards that the recipient will keep forever.

I used to hand write every card. But that took so much time that I only sent cards to select contacts. Of the five business cards I received at an event, only the top two would receive a card. Plus, finding a card that stands out isn't easy.

Now I use an online card sending system that lets me create unique, killer cards on my keyboard, and I still use my own handwriting font and signature.

I scan the contact's business card on my printer/scanner/fax machine and upload the jpeg to the system. I then spend about two minutes creating the cover and content and adding the address for the envelope.

The cover shows a hand holding their business card. It sounds simple but it delivers an impact when the contact opens the envelope to see a greeting card with their own business card on the front.

My inside content is simple-something like:
"I enjoyed meeting you at the chamber event this morning. I'm impressed with your success. I wish we had more time to talk. Let's look for each other at future events."

Simple, complimentary, and focused on the contact. Sending cards like this one is my strongest marketing tool. The cards cost me less than a buck each but they really deliver.

If you don't know someone using SendOutCards and want to send a couple of sample cards at my expense, go to http://go2468.com/cards.

Voice mails rarely get retrieved, emails usually get deleted, but greeting cards get read and displayed.

Good News Summary

1. Follow up need not require selling skills nor pressure.

2. Spend less than a dollar to make a great impression.

Chapter Eight

Other Immediate Follow Up

Following the pleasant conversation and sending them a greeting card, I want to find other ways to enhance my business relationship with my contact. The best way I've found to do that is to look for more common ground. Does this person share any interests, friends, or background with me that we didn't uncover in our initial ten minute chat.

I search their profile on LinkedIn to find more common ground. Here I can see their current or past jobs, their co-workers who have profiles on LinkedIn, where they went to school, in what organizations they have membership, and their hobbies and interests.

It only takes three to four minutes to check their profile to find common ground. If I find something that we share, I make a note of it. This will serve as comfortable opening conversation when we meet again.

If I hit it off particularly well with a contact, I'll invite her to be my connection on LinkedIn. This allows us to keep up with each other. When she changes employers, gets a promotion, or makes any announcements on LinkedIn I'll be notified.

Also, when she and I become LinkedIn connections we can see each others' connections. So I can now look through her list and see whom she knows that I know well. That gives us more common ground and more comfortable chatting subjects.

Good News Summary

1. LinkedIn is a free and quick way to find more common ground.

Chapter Nine

One-on-One Meetings

As you look over your contacts, a few of them will stand out as good referral sources. With some of these you can seek referrals with one-on-one meetings. They may share client niches that compliment yours. For instance, insurance agents love to connect with realtors. So do mortgage brokers, home repair companies, and bankers.

Once you identify a good referral source for you, do the research discussed earlier to find common ground. Check their LinkedIn profile and their company website. Make notes of the areas you share in common.

Ten minutes of research should suffice.
I prefer casual sites for my one-to-one meetings-- coffee shops, cafes, and public areas after a meeting we both attend.

As you begin your visit, explore the areas of common ground you discovered in your research. Start with the people you both know. Those connections are the strongest.

Ask them lots of questions. Here are some important pieces of information I like to find out:

- Who are ideal prospects for them?

- What do they offer that sets them apart from others of their industry?

- What challenges are they facing?

- Do they need the services of any of my other business friends?

Take notes. They'll be impressed and you'll want this information later.

As you listen, think of your network of friends. Who could use this person's services? Who of your friends could help him with his challenges?

Collect a brochure or other material that describes his offerings.

Once you've worn out your ears listening to your new friend, now you can discuss your business. As you tell your contact about yourself, help him understand how you set yourself apart from others. Stress the differences.

Make sure you describe your ideal prospect. Explore the possibility that your clients may be prospects for him and vice versa.

If you feel prompted, ask for referrals during your one-on-one. I've given you my suggestions for asking for referrals in the next chapter.

Use this meeting primarily to continue growing your goodwill.

Following Up
When you return to your office, review your notes. If you're like me you'll have to interpret your notes because of poor handwriting. Do this as early as possible while you can still remember the conversation.

Try to find some way to serve your new friend. Can you refer business to him? Can you find an article that addresses one of his challenges? Is there a book you can recommend?

Send these quickly. Your follow up service doesn't have to be about business. If he loves the Red Sox, send him an e-mail the next time they win. Acknowledge his passion.

Your one-on-one meeting and follow up can deepen your business relationship.

Good News Summary

1. Your contacts will welcome new appointments with you because you made them feel good.

2. A little research gives you the common ground in which you can nurture your relationship.

3. Your follow up after a one-to-one visit bears even more fruit.

Chapter Ten

Attracting Referrals

The object of your business networking efforts is referrals. You don't rub shoulders with other networkers to sell to them. You get to know them so you can trade qualified referrals.

To this point, you've met new people, had pleasant conversations that built goodwill, followed up gently to enhance your goodwill, met with them one-on-one and grew your goodwill some more.

This process has been called farming--planting seeds, nourishing the soil, keeping out the weeds, and then harvesting the fruit.

You've set the stage, now you can reap the rewards. If you've prepared your contacts well enough, the referrals are as easy to reach as low hanging fruit.

Give Before You Ask
The key to receiving lots of referrals is to give lots of referrals. Become a connector.

This may seem illogical and a huge time commitment. But I assure you, it's true.

The key to receiving lots of referrals is to give lots of referrals. Become a connector.

If you give someone a referral without strings or expectations of reciprocation, she will likely return the favor.

I try to give two or three quality referrals a week. I'm always on the look out for people to connect.

My friend Gerry Phelan calls this, "I know a guy marketing."

When you consciously watch for connection opportunities they easily appear.

Each week those I've connected send me thank cards and e-mails. When thanked, I always say, "I'm glad I could. I know you'd do the same for me."

This response gets them thinking about which of their connections would be good matches for me.

Try it. It works.

Asking for Referrals
When you've established a strong relationship with

your new friend and have given her a referral, article, or helped her solve some challenge, you can feel good about asking for referrals.

Most people have trouble coming up with someone for you. But if you're specific about your ideal prospect, you will jog your friend's mind.

Here's an example for my own business:

"I'm looking for any association or business group who wants to assist their folks in attracting more clients. They'll need a speaker to entertain them while teaching them low-cost but fruitful marketing techniques."

Does that bring to mind anyone in your network? If so, e-mail me at david@daviddeford.com.

When your friend gives you a referral, follow up with the referral within 24 hours. Send a thank you card as soon as you follow up and report how it went.

Referrals are the fruit and networking is the farming process. Improve the process and gather more fruit.

Good News Summary

1. Setting the stage for reaping referrals is simple.

2. Give before you ask.

3. Asking is easy once you've given referrals to your friend.

Chapter Eleven

Success Is Certain

I told you the process was simple. It's also amazingly fruitful.

Creating and nurturing goodwill feels good and helps you attract quality referrals.

It's clear and simple.
Have pleasant conversations; Send a follow up card;
Find common ground;
Give before you ask;
Meet one-on-one;
Continue giving value;

I told you I had good news.

If you follow the principles in this book, success is certain.

I'd love to tell your success stories in an upcoming book. Send them to me at david@daviddeford.com.

I wish you every success.

Resources

For a full list of resources with easy links go to www.DavidDeFord.com/resources.

Beals, Jeff, *Self Marketing Power: Branding Yourself as a Business of One*. Omaha: Keynote Publishing, LLC, 2008.

Burg, Bob, *Endless Referrals: Network Your Everyday Contacts into Sales*. New York: McGrawHill, 2006.
Ferrazzi, Keith, Never Eat Alone: And Other Secrets to Success, One Relationship at a Time. New York: Doubleday, 2005.

Gitomer, Jeffrey, *Little Black Book of Connections: 6.5 Assets for Networking Your Way to Rich Relationships*. Austin: Bard Press, 2006.

Mackay, Harvey, *Dig Your Well Before You're Thirsty*. New York: Doubleday, 1997.

Misner, Ivan R., *Masters of Networking: Building Relationships for Your Pocketbook and Soul*. Atlanta: Bard Press, 2000.

Templeton, Tim, The Referral of a Lifetime: The Networking System That Produces Bottom-Line Results Every Day! San Francisco: Berrett-Koehler Publishers, Inc., 2004.

Vermeiren, Jan, Let's Connect: A Practical Guide for Highly
Effective Professional Networking. New York:
Morgan-James, 2008.